VISITING
RITES

PRINCETON SERIES OF CONTEMPORARY POETS

For Other Books in the Series, see page 84

VISITING RITES

by Phyllis Janowitz

Princeton University Press
Princeton, New Jersey

Copyright © 1982 by Princeton University Press

Published by Princeton University Press, 41 William Street,
Princeton, New Jersey 08540

In the United Kingdom: Princeton University Press, Guildford, Surrey

Publication of this book has been aided by a grant from
the Paul Mellon Fund of Princeton University Press

This book has been composed in Linotron Sabon

Clothbound editions of Princeton University Press books
are printed on acid-free paper, and binding materials are
chosen for strength and durability

Printed in the United States of America by Princeton
University Press, Princeton, New Jersey

Designed by Laury A. Egan

Library of Congress Cataloging in Publication Data

Janowitz, Phyllis.
Visiting rites.

(Princeton series of contemporary poets)
I. Title.   II. Series.
PS3560.A534V5   811'.54   82-47601
ISBN 0-691-06523-3   AACR2
ISBN 0-691-01398-5 (pbk.)

"Case" (p. 3); © 1980 The New Yorker Magazine, Inc.
"Waiting for Father in Pawling, N.Y." (pp. 67-68);
© 1981 The New Yorker Magazine, Inc.

for A. R. Ammons

Contents

Acknowledgments

The Anthology of Magazine Verse and Yearbook of American Poetry, 1981, for "Case"

The Best of the Radcliffe Quarterly for "The Grandmothers are Getting Younger"

Beyond Baroque for "*Nacht Musik*" and "Solitude"

Connections for "Minuet in a Minor Key"

The Devil's Millhopper for "Unraveling," "Keeping Time," and "*Nacht Musik*"

Esquire for "The Warm House is a Sanctuary" (originally published in a slightly different version as "Night Watch")

The John O'Hara Journal for "Cells," winner of the 1981 poetry prize, "Fisherman's Wife," and "Liberty"

The National Forum for "Celebration" and "Music of Stars and Wheels"

The New American Review for "Synechdoche by the Beautiful Sea" and "Tone Poem for the Spring of the Year"

The New Republic for "Jitters"

The New Yorker for "Case" and "Waiting for Father in Pawling, N.Y."

Ploughshares for "The Apple Tree and Mrs. Lucky Enter Winter Together," "Mrs. Lucky," published under the title "Although I am Taking Courses," and "Visiting Rites"

Prairie Schooner for "The Fisherman," published under the title "Giant Step," "Roles," and "Sardines"

The Radcliffe Quarterly for "The Grandmothers are Getting Younger"

The Raintree Press for "The Party" and "Promises" (limited edition broadsides)

Ubu #3 for "Cygnet" and "Home"

Ubu #4 for "Baptism at Stow Lake," "Facts and Figures," and "Rejects"

Willow Springs for "Pickling"

Woman Poet for "Compensations," Published under the title "Mrs. Lucky"

"Cells" received the Bernice Ames Award from the Poetry Society of America, 1978

"Electronic Capriccio for Solo Electron" received the Celia B. Wagner Award from the Poetry Society of America, 1980

"Film" received the Lucille Medwick Award from the Poetry Society of America, 1981

"Fisherman's Wife" received the Consuelo Ford Award from the Poetry Society of America, 1980

"Juice" received the Consuelo Ford Award from the Poetry Society of America, 1982

With my gratitude to Princeton University for the Alfred Hodder Fellowship in the Humanities which made it possible for me to write a number of these poems and to put this collection into its present form.

1

Case

This is a tale of the body, its inert
material, sullen texture, which I do
not understand. Passive and massive it is
tedious, tedious, as it sits in a

fatherly armchair, refusing to get up
to look for its slippers and the day's paper.
While the mind is no doubt worrying about
how bloated and repulsive the body is

becoming and wondering why it doesn't
care to rise and jog several times around
the block in the rain. The mind thinks, Without a
body hair would not need to be blown dry, chins

squared, eyebrows lifted and so forth. All of us
could thus and in such a manner have more time.
This is a marriage between a drugged slug and
an aerial acrobat. The mind has more

than once applied for divorce, but the body
doesn't want to be bothered with procedures.
The body wants to be left alone to sit
in the sun's way and to spread, like some kind of

vegetable matter, into the loam of the
garden. The mind would like to strangle it, but
lacks that kind of strength. Oh no, this is not a
blissful coupling! Often the mind is as quick

as some sprightly animal traveling by
way of hanging vines with all the ancestral
energy the body lacks, in its torpor,
waiting for supper, the smell of food raking
through its middle like a red-hot fingernail.

Mrs. Lucky

Although I am taking courses in the language
of children, penguin socialization
and creative writing, now, in my dotage—

dotage, what a striking word—I find
myself betrayed—betrayed—by what?
Betrayed! That's what it means to be human.

First acceptance, then rage, then reiteration.
Once dinner was always exactly at seven.
We said a prayer. Naturally, I imagined

my grandchildren would have red hair and make
kipful good as my own. I didn't think they'd
arrive right off the green farms of Alpha Centauri

out of touch, wearing headphones and refusing
to move without tape decks and wide receivers.
Exhausting, their tolerance for a drifting world.

How can I get through to them? Listen, listen
I want to say (as if it would make a difference)
without order there can be no love, not even

tenderness, the only possible purpose
under a dying sun—the only one.
My hearing grows worse with the years;

what passes from human to human is inaudible,
yet how clearly I hear what they hear. Fragile
and pale, Humpty-Dumpty bounces on his wall

in the sky, high on the timeliest twaddling tunes
and worlds may break to bits, worlds may be reglued.
I nod and sigh. What else can I do?

It is not to me, alone, the little
angels cry, *Come to dust Come to dust*
The sun has ten billion years to go.

The Apple Tree and Mrs. Lucky
Enter Winter Together

Trunk, branches, leaves—
sere and blemished—
I am not what I wanted.

Dignity is a hindrance.
I am weighted with notions
and unbalanced by fear.

Night sweats, vapours.
Why am I frightened
alone on the street?

No one is here—
a pair of brown squirrels—
a few fallen apples—

These rococo grimaces, sequins
and pearls of despair—baubles
suitable for someone younger.

It is time to shed them,
to remove in artful fashion
the accumulated trinkets,

the scarves, hats and sashes,
the *maquillage*, the foliage,
the peacock plumage of my years.

While some brassy music blares
I shall peel, first, my kidskin
gloves, then send layer after

layer packing—faille chemise
and skirt, clocked stockings—
fling garters to the breeze,

skillfully teasing, and strip
what remains, until a few sparse
feathers are all I have to wear.

The lights dim. The last leaves
descend. And I? Ha! I shall blow
kisses, go with the wind, pin up

my threads of hair and pretend
a composed smile has always been
carved on my face, this peace

in my eyes is not merely a pose
and growing old—something
to look forward to.

Compensations

I have reached the right age. Speeding
adrenal molecules no longer skid
through my veins wearing crash helmets

and goggles like Mario Andretti.
Now they go in for a beer; they walk.
Or they take the local, hanging onto

a strap, reading *People* magazine
through bifocals. They forget to get
off at their stop. For whole hours,

maybe days, I am able to reassure
the young when their faces turn
blue with tears. Mick Jagger.

Mercedes Benzes. Gucci, Pucci.
Who cares? Whatever we get we
keep such a short time it doesn't

matter. I say this over. Often
pebbles are left in the sifter.
I'm old enough to stop such playing.

What can I buy with pebbles?
Another pint of blood?
There are compensations for blood

gone thin. I've put up
fences and locked myself in
with a tin of tea, a telescope

full of old stars. Once
our heads barely reached the sill,
the candy machine turned

and turned, heavy and slow:
pink blue green—
hard lumps to suck but ocean sweet

as long as the last sticky pieces
stuck to our teeth. Now the flowers
darken and dry in their clear flask—

the legacy of summer. Sores won't
heal anymore. Something wants to cut
loose; something is trying to tear.

Anyone can see through me, hear
the liquids filter through my veins.
Muddy gravy. Tin can jello.

Overheated radiators, spitting blood.
Oh cold kiss approaching, sweeter than
any I've ever had, your breath smells

like the milk of my mother! Cheer-
leaders should chant elegies outside
my window. Give me a D, give me a D,

give me a D D D! I live on credit
in my final cell and it isn't good.
One gets used to bruised veins but not

the bills, or those hospital religiosos
steeped in recycled words, equating
indifference with the will of God.

Games and Refrains of Children

1. *Sardines*

The baby is not exceedingly miserable.
Its bleat signifies, rather, a refusal.
It will not willingly accept betrayal.

What could it want? Does it have croup, catarrh?
It sings its sorrowful song from breakfast to supper
and vice versa. The frail notes convene and warble

from a vent above Letitia's self-cleaning oven.
She would like to complain, but no one can tell
her where an infant—possibly orphaned—

is roosting. Perhaps, in the wall, a cradle
is endlessly rocking a small, unblissful baby.
Perhaps it is merely a Platonic ideal,

the essential quintessence of infancy.
It might be the voice of the next generation.
There are other voices, Letitia insists.

When she wakes she does not wake alone.
She looks around. She is the only one
in bed. Yet it's crowded, there is no room.

Covering her is a blanket of arguments,
demands, threats and regrets. This is existence
in a grand new complex. She doesn't know

what to do with the imps of exuberance
cavorting about her head, cartwheeling over
her stomach, the noise in the walls growing louder,

and no one to take a complaint, issue a citation,
and no one to say what is tangible, what is not—
no one with any substance or conviction.

2. *Roles*

Herman would make an impeccable baby,
even a believable brother, the kind
easily scalped by Indians, the kind

who might rise to command squadrons
of Samurai warriors. But a father
is not John Wayne, Elvis Presley,

or Ilie Nastase. A father leaves
with a passionless kiss and returns
with a daily paper, circles of sweat

ringing his armpits. It is true,
nevertheless, that he has not
always been this dull, this careful,

he can remember the bliss of tropical
tantrums, the moist exotic anguish
blooming over a bitter cheekbone,

a listless air, a lack of delicacy
in the touch of lover or friend.
Why is it he, once adored for twitching

instability and astonished hair—
often compared to a porcupine's quills—
yes, why, when they come bearing tales

of infantile quarrels, is it he who must
halve the baby, smiling benevolently,
his rage like underwear under the bed,

pushed out of sight, but highly compressed,
even dense, and unpredictable as a sudden
hole in a sky leafed with vertigo.

Letitia and Prue

1. Unraveling

This is our room; the clothes
on the floor have been worn,
but not by us. They date
back before our time. A few

belonged to Aunt Hannalke, who
lived nearby in a hunting lodge
with three starving greyhounds.
They left permanent pawprints

on her summer frocks and bitten
scars on her arms. When she died
we received a box of sleeveless
dresses and a box of sleeves.

Our nightmares are epiphanies
of connections. This aqua
taffeta with the tight skirt
is a Balenciaga (circa 1950).

This peach *mousseline*, weighted
with sequins, must have been
chosen by some raucous pip-
squeak to do the Charleston in.

And friend fox, with his fixed,
lunatic eyes, has to be cleaned
and given a new tail; we'd do
well if we sold him now—

but we never would, we'd
rather sell our brother, only
he's dead. These jars contain
morsels of broken glass we

put in our shoes if we wish to walk.
Collectors of the rare and obscure
must approach impossible borders
where the body cannot go,

where a black-veiled wind tears
around on a bicycle, where the air
is so pure breathing is like
swallowing fire. Which explains

the swollen ankles of that lump
you hear snoring on beaded pillows,
mascara caking her eyes, my bouts
of pleurisy, steaming tea kettles,

and why we prefer to stay in bed
surrounded by a plethora of books
and antique mannequins, our quest
holy as anyone's, letting the door-

bell ring until it dies, until
silence returns in fogs and ethers,
wearing the clothes of historical
figures or former friends.

2. Hide and Seek

Wearing a torn undershirt, Millard Fillmore
surfaces in the mirror. From his lower
lip a hook dangles like a cigarette.

Letitia glimpses something lethal she was not
scheduled to see. Memory—a disconnected
entity longing for connections—selects

its messages nervously, plays partial chords
in a minor key. Then a few major ones,
gilded patches on an aging tapestry. Tapestry.

The word preserves drafty winters, thermostats
set at sixty degrees, lavender and moody
piano tunes; catches faces in threadbare

drawing rooms; veined ivory hands pass cups,
butter dishes, silver sugar spoons. Viewed
this way, years shrink to a single Sunday

afternoon, a lethargic dog scratching a flea.
Is she never to be rid of this persona,
this unicorn leaping miniature hedges,

browsing on meringues glacés and sugary tea?
Her face spills, spreading like honey,
settles into jowels, the nose curls up—

a corkscrew. Victoria Regina raises a lorgnette
with monarchial glee. An eyeblink later, one
views George Washington, stern above the chin,

cloudy in the lower echelons. Daily occurrences.
Is anyone home? Cells in flux, moths capriciously
circling a gas lamp. No one permanent.

3. Nacht Musik

How simple it is when men put on their
hats and promenade the luminous

evenings of summer. Cows dance over
moons, numismatic pockets quiver,

blood shivers in hidden veins,
private women peer between the blinds.

How simple it is when men meet in cafés.
(Only a skinny kicked cat complains.)

They wear their simple birthrights like
shiny gold watches on long gold chains.

Poppets and palmettoes, so ethereal,
stir the night air, and shadowy blues

and mangoes are also delicate,
while somewhere a cicada purrs,

I wish I wish I wish I wish,
persistent as the bliss of stars.

4. Pickling

For hours we painstakingly skin and bone
the herring. Tenderly we arrange them

in gallon jars, cover with vinegar
and pungent pickling spices. Now once more

we are friends, euphoric, performing this
kuchen rite. We bake zucchini bread. Bliss!

And unearth old albums. Our likenesses
are sprouting raised white spots. Nevertheless

we're recognizable. It's possible
our blemishes, like mosquito bites, will

heal and vanish. We will return to our
tufted youth. We kiss. It might be better

just to look. But looking is not enough.
Small fish, undone, turn to dust at our touch.

5. Nesting

Home is where we're free to be our
sickest, you and I, a permanent *malaise,*

mal à la tête, folie à deux, all of that
and more. You with your plumed straw

hat you wear in bed; I in my "layered"
outfit with leg-of-mutton sleeves,

bringing you nourishing tid-bits:
a cold fritter, a slice of pale gold

Swiss cheese with the rind removed,
a jar of Mister Mustard. We do get on!

I hear my No-Cal, a cricket in its
plastic cup, it sits on the back of

a writing pad, singing its little
fizzy song, telling me to drink

it up, quick, before it goes flat,
like you, under your cover of blue

all old and flat and stale, and only
the curled green feather sticking out.

6. *Waving*

You in your bed I in mine. Flip,
flip, the pages of our books are turning.

We are at another station, impatiently
waiting for the pulse of the machine to

begin ticking once more. Uncurl the toes?
Impossible! Blood backs in the brain

like the sea, foaming whitely; any move
will be the wrong one. Before us an empty

breadboard soon will be full, we will be
making sandwich after sandwich, always

18

too slowly, always more hands reaching.
We will be mashing butter into choppy

lumps, smearing it on wheat and rye.
Then the long, drunken trip through

careening cars, "Ham chicken or cheese!
Ham chicken or cheese!" New Orleans.

London. Buenos Aires. Eau Claire,
Wisconsin. All such imaginative places,

reeking of cindery books. Galsworthy
and Melville. Dreiser. Tarkington.

We read with half a mind.
The right half—somewhere else.

7. Keeping Time

If there are answers they do
not arrive on the first of May,
singing from your door knob,

pink heads, green grasses
sprouting up. If there are
answers they arrive when

the geraniums have lost all
color, ill from lack of water
and the exhaust. Nothing will

revive them. If there are
answers, Biscuit will find them
first. He will drag them outside.

When you open the door
bits of stuffing will rise
and whiten the blossoming plum.

8. *September*

September is a beginning, the steam of summer
rolling south. Much activity. All their lives

they have been preparing; now they speed up.
Drawers rattle. Closets are shoeless, floors
impeccable. The canary is given away,

carpets put in storage, the lawn mowed
one final time. Letitia moves to a small
apartment; she fills all 3 rooms with spindly

furniture and china figurines. When visitors
come she pours tea with lemon into thin cups
sprigged with flowers. She says, "In the blue

vase. I think. Daisies." Decomposing phrases,
as if she has lost some fundamental glue.

Visiting Rites

We drive up the winding road
lined by graying sycamores,
a blessing in the summer heat.

At a small table, between
the stones, a man and two women
nibble crustless sandwiches,

pour from a silver pot of tea.
They have their arrangements:
dour frigidity of gladioli,

faded dresses, a musty gentility.
We have brought a few daisies,
short-lived and casual.

It's a matter of style, Mother says.
Days of water, days of sun put
circles in the trees. A green-

glass summer lies in pieces. It is
afternoon. We watch the women
pack their picnic away. Counting

Live, die, live, die,
Mother assigns white petals
to a mound of earth. Something

hidden but familiar will repeat
the same design—it is not
a question of illness or cure.

If I could refuse such whispers,
such sighs, I'd fold the long
shawls of mourning, give up

descendants, prayer—all
kinds of fixed hooks—be single
as an angel, dancing and blind.

The Grandmothers are Getting Younger

The grandmothers are getting younger,
rock more swiftly on curving spines.
Something is happening to those faces,
thin and white as rice paper
with all the words of their lives drawn across.

They are changing into Chinese dancers,
bent brush strokes
giving themselves to the wind.
Oh how beautiful the grandmothers
are growing younger and their lips
move and their eyes are silver.
The dust covers taken off,
and underneath it is clear
as early day and all the rust
and old moss removed.

Look! Their hair is thicker and the gray
is going away. They run
across empty spaces to meet
someone in the long wet grass,
young as young girls who laugh
as they run, throwing sweaters
and shawls down in white heaps.
The leaves of their voices rise,
floating up, and fasten
to branches like wings turning green.

The Soul has no Morality

We do not hear the hooves,
Although they grow louder, hourly,
And the horses are magnificent,
Snooty and vain!
And the carriage is black and stately.

The soul has no morality.
It is waiting, fidgety with hope.
It is too abstract to escape,
And not clever at all.
It is no Houdini.

The train takes its time.
At each stop there are mourners
Weeping and waving.
The soul does not weep.
It has no sense of what is proper.

The soul is not even near the train!
On another galaxy it listens to horns.
It whirls on pins. It is clapping
Restless hands. It is singing
"Blue Moon" off key.

$\underline{\underline{2}}$

Promises

Only a handful of them, really dust.
They just can't last forever.
Too many vibrations from passing
trucks, too many sonic booms
and their patterns will shatter
like flowers of glass.

But see how they are admired,
placed and spaced on beds of cotton.
We are careful, bending over,
not to lean on the cases. O
look at the upright
consonants and the vowels
sway and break
into bloom.

Surely there's something here
that's meant for us
to take away, a fragrance,
a spurt of color, that will last
at least as long
as hyacinths.

Music of Stars and Wheels

On top of nine mattresses an egg
is spinning. Long before the hour
of conception, deception begins.

It is not unexpected. Then comes
the hour of naming, the gathering
of kin, sweet Burgundies, pastries

in frilled bonnets; and the babies, wet
and furious in their long lace gowns.
Grandma's feelings are hurt, Aunt Jennie

is slighted, Cousin Morton is leaving.
Mrs. Keskey weeps in the kitchen. Sun
and moon have nothing to do with these

attitudes fixed by rage or isolation.
This confusion, this weight of decision
is up to the distant stars, their

outgoing positions in the firmament,
tongues dying to tell their tale.
At the proper moment those assigned

guardian-angel roles ring the bell.
They smell of cold air, whiskey
and cologne. They bring toys cloaked

in thick gold paper. Even they do not
know which packages are their own,
which wrappings conceal the truck

that will break an axle, the train track
warped at the joinings, sharp edges sticking
up for the children to rip their hearts on.

The Contagious Hospital

Life at the heights
requires a certain
aversion. We turn
our faces away

when we pass other
windows. "Draw
the curtains," we fret
—not out loud—

even for our thoughts
someone could shoot
us dead.
Next door Stephen

Foster in a minor
key is practicing
the mandolin. And on
a superior floor

a reconditioned tuba
gushes, falters and dies.
This is not a musical
dwelling, this high-

cost housing with its
drilling hive of eyes,
hum and thrum,
Sturm und Drang.

We don't wish to complain.
So many are homeless,
sleep in the rain, live
on rice-grains and water.

The purpose of our hand-
hooked words merely
to clarify, escape illusion.
Each unit contains:

two highstrung children,
a wailing baby with lungs
of Pittsburgh steel,
a TV with indigestion,

a rabbit-coated poodle—
each apartment
one molecule of this typical
arrangement we call "home."

Home

At the dinner table forks
and knives fall heavily
upon us. This is uncomfortable.

Bony fish. Chopped eggshell
soufflé. Sandy cookies.
We chew and chew. If charity

begins at home, we are on the moon,
looking through the wrong
end of a kaleidoscope,

all our crusty furniture
coming and going. The records,
stored in the basement, warped.

A waltz, moaning on the turn-table,
skewered like live meat, while
our beefy baby rocks and roars.

We hope to exchange him at Sears.
He is not what we paid for.
We think his components are rusty.

At the bureau we bequeath our several
parts. In London or Larchmont
someone who insistently awaits

our departure is dialing. Somebody
needs a stomach, an eye, a heart.
Soon someone will hear the good news.

A man will arrive with a Kirby
to vacuum dead skin from our bed.
The world will look grisly.

No one will care.
Even at our pickled table the air
will not clear.

A stranger, reconditioned, will
chew on fingers and toes and duck
low flying silverware.

The Party

Something speechless wants to say
something. *I am. I am. I am.* Or,

making its way around each couple,
How nice for him! How nice for her!

And then wave a glass at the room.
But where is a suitcase of smiles

for something speechless, who lives
in a cloudy peat bog with no flowers;

who each day waters a garden of eggplants,
and each day walks the dog? Who wants

to say, It is like This! It is like That!
Who wants to discuss Trade Agreements

and the *National Enquirer.* Whose eyes
in the morning grow darker; who at night

dreams of crowds weeping and fainting
beneath whizzing combustible words.

Tone Poem for the Spring of the Year

1

Stubby Janina spends
her days dusting cans
of tunas, jars of dill.

Dull as ragweed. Shivery
jellies for a treat. Certainly
nothing is less boring to eat.

Spring has come to that bit
of acreage labeled a yard.
The grass is beginning to sprout.

Soon she will need to mow it.
She knows she should watch her weight.
And the cat. Should she shampoo it?

She reclines on a Barca-lounge
sipping iced tea, regarding
her feet, brushing away

an infinitesimal gnat.
Snails cling like burrs to the flat
green leaves of the portulaca.

She pokes at one of the spirals
finding a passageway into
a room where life is sweet

without chocolate cake. A widening
crack reveals a naked
child bedecked with snail

shells, clutching a rattle,
a molecule of matter
with a guarantee, who will

not remember its birthing
or the nine long months before.
In impractical gardens of sand

and Colubrina, not pondering
possible pitfalls or the role
it has been assigned, mindless,

it will wait to mate,
expand, and with great delight
reproduce its kind.

2

She thinks she is mutable as
snow becomes rain
and the light unbandages a single
scrawny lilac

earlier each morning.
The dog pees on her book.
Janina laughs,
one white square

is missing from her mouth
like a note of music.
Is she the mother,
day by day

melting into an old woman
toothless and furious,
with everyone broken to house-ways,
their orderly

bones picked up,
or is she the daughter
unzipping a warm
ridiculous joke? She must

choose among possibilities
indifferent as roses
moulting after their season,
while another heavy-

lidded growth composes
itself above them
mournfully intoning,
"What to do? What to do?"

3

The warm house is a sanctuary
for crickets and moths.
Trapped in thick sheets,

shaking up from darkness,
Jennie imagines a plague
of falling frogs, incipient

volcanoes under the front lawn,
the neighbor's dog berserk
and foaming. She checks

clocks and doors, smooths
sheets and follows the cat
all night on his track

through cellars and ratholes,
counting possibilities that hang
like huge wings upside down.

When no one is watching, tidal waves
swallow whole families. Sometimes
the bodies are never recovered.

Only Jennie's flashlight keeps
the tide back, the fortune-teller's
prophecy of drowning unfulfilled.

4

The violets on her dresser
have bleached and dried together—
small bones left from summer.
Hours and days can be threaded

through the veins of a mosquito,
or trapped in the eye of a fly.
What she remembers spreads
over years, a lowering sky.

More soft-spoken than in her
forties, Janina pours
milk for the cat, watches
with the detachment of a vestal

virgin as he loquaciously laps.
How extremely pleasant
it is, she is
a prisoner of the assorted

senses no more. Each day
is a story with a hackneyed
plot, deftly wrapped,
no fear of dropped lines,

and the heart, rocking steady—
a ship called *Docility*.
She times the seasons,
cutting the year into

quarters like a pie,
with the fixed precision
of a cafeteria chef.
It is possible she will

someday repeat the cycles—
longing, love, rejection, even
death. She looks forward,
majestic as a lion, her yawn.

Rejects

"We must love one another and die,"
Letitia said, giving me her
diary to ponder. She hopped like
a child with kitchen utensils

from pot cover to potato masher.
What I wanted was only a few
minutes to observe the world
through her fragile, painted eyes

and then to re-enter the untidy
nest of my own body, its
singular derision. My need
not to question and listen, or

to imagine, but to *be* Letitia,
only I wondered if I could really
return after knowing, with nerves
and skin, with veins beneath

the skin, capillaries, the smallest
finger-joints; after that fleshy
knowledge no person or thing would be
the same—the mind, temporary

and trapped in its enclosure,
the heart, fluttering until it stops
numbly fixed against the chest wall
and blind in all its beauty.

Facts and Figures

Over our very heads is a magic
show of hocus-pocus and chimera.
Streams of stars have been dead
for years; they shine and quiver

like clusters of phosphorescent
fish, Letitia said, while one
night's gaze is not enough
to ascertain if the moon

is waxing or waning, although
it is a clear night
and the rotund circle is
almost complete. Letitia didn't

learn this in school, or that
men are hard and flat as
numbers, yet singular, or that
it takes two to make one.

She will imagine a baby,
a toothless red mouth and a howl.
Newborn it will look like a pig.
She will allow no illusions.

She will give up her imaginary
plan for driving a subway
through measureless caverns
while moonlighting at Dunkin

Donuts, dipping heavy
crullers into honey, dusting
powdered sugar from her hands.
Or she will not imagine a baby.

The frantic creature, like so many
others, will never be born.
Whatever she does will be wrong.
She finds this odd fact comforting.

Fisherman's Wife

By the side of the lake where last summer
the drowned man was hooked, the lilacs,

pale silver, filigreed, weighted
with perfume, tremble without concern.
In their rented bungalows the lake

dwellers, equally indifferent
wait for warmer weather, the drowning
forgotten that last summer supplied

a suitable object for the passion
no one would admit to. Not I—not you.
Blue lake, two people, the air blurred

between them. Sinkers tied like bells,
wrists and ankles, sinkers around
my waist. I was not alone

when I prepared for the sounding
and not alone when I went under.
They pulled up one, they pulled up two

stone blue, wound with fish-line and reeds.
I coughed and shook the water from
my ears, painted two bloody moons

on my cheeks—you, gasping, a great
blotchy fish, wanted only to stay
at the bottom, steeped in that brackish

pond, me, hooked in your arms, sun snaking
the surface, no shadows between us.

The Fisherman

Too gargantuan for the apartment,
he has tried, great stalking creature,
to make himself shrink. Furniture

creaks and strains; beneath him
the velvet loveseat sinks.
His head cracks against doorframes.

His eyes, anesthetized, are stuck
in their crisis. This is the regulated
life, the neat, acceptable wife

he put on reserve years before,
hum of an immaculate vacuum, just
what he wanted. Now it is the bush

country of his old fear he remembers
and needs. Crocodile gape,
leopard crouch, flush of epinephrine—

brown teeth scraping his cheek,
gamy breath in his face. Unless
he is forced to push the apparition

away in a bloody tussle of love,
the day deranges nothing
but trash-fish and a mangy dog.

He lopes off, guided by the string
he is tied to and a whistle
high above the shrunken human range.

Fisherman's Wife #2

What I wanted, all I wanted,
I said, was time. Which concern
you gave me. Tick tick
Tick tick Tick tick Tick tick.

The sound of the sea
in a velvet box. Displeased,
I flung the Phillipe Patek—
or whatever it was—to the floor

and stamped on it. Time?
I said, hopping about on
whichever foot wasn't bleeding.
I wanted love and adoration.

That kind of thing. Get out
and don't come back without.
You danced away—the salt
of the sea. Crabs danced

after you, sun needles pricking
your bubbles your shadows
your spine. The moon—an old
woman wrapped in plush clouds—

stopped at the top of its roller-
coaster tracks, leapt from the sky
and landed on my lap, a great moon-
baby: wild, bald, and demanding from

me, alone, the world. Snail spirals
parted, cones of paper flowers
spilled, houses warped with moss
swung loose their doors. What does

one do with a strange, squalling
brat? Sweet clam I claimed him
eye of the folding limpet.
I held him, rocked him, and I wept.

Minuet in a Minor Key

Almost touching, almost joining, two
cars come together in a slow
dance beside a roadside inn. No one

watches as a woman in blue transfers
a young boy like a blown-glass
vase from the rusted yellow Mustang

into a vermilion Pinto driven by
a bearded and impatient man. The sun
slips from the sky, a burning city

stealing color from the clustering bodies,
turning them into vapors. Both cars
flee the dark in opposing trajectories

the way fireflies on a summer night
evade small hands and the collecting jar.
Two evenings later a reunion is witnessed

by the same stucco structure with its
mournful orange roof; the boy is changed
from red to yellow, as if a magician's

wand had control of his spectrum.
Engines spin once more, the speeding
cars recede in opposite directions,

taking no notice of posted limits or
signs of treacherous soft shoulders,
frost heaves ahead.

Electronic Capriccio for Solo Electron

1. Gregory: Fantasia

People disturb him, gliding
in rhythms he cannot
shift into. A weather map
drawn by someone deranged
makes his pulse uneven,
the winds of his forecasts
swiftly change.

He practices daily, *jetés,*
entrechats, but it astounds him,
this dance arranged
by an alien choreographer,
the erratic designs
he prints on the floor.

The valves in his veins
swing open and shut,
the blood spurt starting
and stopping.
He walks or leaps.
He's a crow. Then a wing
drags on the ground
and he limps.

He speeds up, slows down,
tries to weave into the crowd,
but at his own rate, in clouds
he winds around him;
only his eyes slice through.
He wants no one
to notice his irregular
gait, no one to brake
the music he moves to.

2. *Staccato*

Rage splashes the bedroom,
blood-red carnations climb
the walls. The king-sized
blanket has dual controls,
twisted somehow—

one side is Hell,
the other Antarctica. Still
the flowers grow into
their sodden splendor.
Gregory cannot change

channels after his
eyes are shut. He is
a principal actor.
He cannot leave until
the show is over,

and the script writers
have stopped their monkey
chatter. He says he
almost never sleeps
more than an hour.

The sheets are sandy.
There are sudden slaps
like the hand of his
mother rising from
the unbled radiator:

footsteps over his head
music   laughter
babies shrieking
ambulances   police
cars chasing the dead.

He cannot remember the crime.
He only knows who
the criminal is and how
much he is charged
for each performance.

3. Sostenuto

A mystery from swaying upper
stories. In a cubicle
white as medicinal waiting
rooms a damp head
pops out of a shell,
wings shudder and spread.

Gregory watches a pigeon
flap from his window,
a message taped to its leg.
Do trees have eyes like office
windows? It flies
low, under girders, under
splayed ceilings of steel.

The last passenger pigeon,
a female, died in Cincinnati.
Gregory can't remember
the telegraph. And sullen
messengers in stiff hats
steering their ships through
traffic. These days volcanoes

can be assembled from a kit.
Who knows what will come by air,
freight light and frail
as the wishbone of a swallow,
a blue fingernail,
the heart of an owl in an envelope.

4. Cantabile

He believes in straight ups and downs, can't
recall flying at night with bat wings
and a kind of radar over mountains
blinded by snow. However it seems he's

awake when he sleeps. Here he is, in France.
Le Jardin des Tuileries.
He cries with joy to be back again.
(In fact he has never been to France.)

His eyes appear open, but he's watching
colors take form, cubes change into circles
dazed by flashing purples and blues. He's
peering through holes in the centers of stars.

Now he asks a stranger to dance. They
waltz as if they're fused to each other.
He remembers meeting her before, when
he was walking on his hands at the beach,

or maybe sitting on top of a tree in
the yard where they once built a house
together. If you ask him a question
he will try to look lively, as if he is

thinking hard. As if the right words are
beyond reach but aware, flickers on
a telephone wire. But your questions
upset the hyena who laughs by the door,

who guards his lost moments, those silvery bands
that keep him from falling, until the old man
shuffles in, the one who shakes him from his
airy denials into the nightmare of morning.

5. Diminuendo

A buttoned vest matching his suit, shoes
reflecting the sun. During the day
he resembles the Gregory his friends

believe resembles them. While each night
a little more air seeps from his electric
blanket like air from a punctured lung,

each minute marked by his digital clock
is colder than the preceding one.
He sleeps on ships caged in ice, trapped

seals turn to stone. The last Eskimo
sets off alone on a raft. Gregory,
his arms nailed to his chest, is lying

supine, waiting for the wind to mail him
to Asia Minor or Kowloon. Becoming part
of rays and monsoons he drifts through

spiny passageways. Only the electric currents
mimicking his own and the bones of his blanket
molded into human form, list the date of arrival.

6. Coda

He cuts himself out, a paper
figure not touching the shore.
However! Touchstones remain,
writing notes, reminding
him of those who succeed in

spite of mothers and fathers.
They suggest executive
positions, Herman Miller
chairs. They invite him
to parties. Are there

no islands for a recluse?
Visitors arrive in canoes.
They wonder what to do
about bears. He rattles some
stones in a jar and sells

them homemade root beer.
In this year of seclusion his
milk-white hair has curdled.
He has never spent one day
in undistracted isolation.

Are there no monasteries
for a heretic? His skyline
is darkened by vast silhouettes.
A helicopter spins low, like
a lost stork over Newark.

3

Dry Soup

How listings and pictures
leak from the tired mind.
Dust thickens the lungs.
Coal dust, sawdust, asbestos paddings.

The islands of Langerhans
drift out of sight and are not
missed. Blanks, clips, transcripts,
folders, requests, bills, wills.

And the gravity of maps
and tacks. Old friends vanish.
New workmen arrive. The heart
does not rock or cavort.

The sky will not drop
a single teasing veil
from its inscrutable wrappings.
And the pigeons, inevitable.

And the new hatchings.
Xerox. Xerox. Xerox.

Liberty

Let me remind you, this pitiful
room on this ship
for the mentally dull

for the numb, for the null
the torpid, the stunned
and those whose nerves

are chipped beyond repair—
where hours whirl, spin
and are smacked about

like diapers in
a wacked-out machine—
mangled and grim, none of them

will ever come clean—
you have chosen
this of your own volition

although your eyes were baked
and your mouth taped shut.
There are infinite

ways of passing go.
There is Bingo.
There are cards.

There are books behind
locked glass doors.
You can lacquer

Cheerios
with nail polish—
string them on strings—

while the phonograph sings
"Oh where have you
been Billy Boy?"

And somewhere an infant
reddens and screams.
You can listen to the twinkle

and snap of cereal
beneath your
horny feet.

You can cut up
the cut ups.
You can beat up the clay.

You can shut
yourself into the bathroom
and pray for the end

of this typical day.
You can sprinkle
arsenic

on the lettuce—
divorce—
remember this:

the possibilities are not
limitless.
They are yours.

Baptism at Stow Lake

FOR CAROL FRANK

A woman in a chenille
dress paddles a canoe, while
bags of babies like footless
seals conceal the narrow

wooden borders of her craft.
Only the heads stick up,
wicked, papery faces
folded like fans. Today

she is taking them out
for a spin. On reaching
the middle she will teach
them to swim. A clone of

the woman who lived in a
shoe with so many children
she grows bitter and confused,
no crony for laughter,

no room for an *au pair*.
At last she knows what to do.
She zips them in baggies
and takes them all with her.

It is Sunday. It is now
or never. And although
she is thirty or over
her face gathers particles—

possibilities—
flecks of light which
rest briefly on her cheeks
before they flutter away.

The faces of the babies
are those of wizened old
women. Their hair is frizzy
or hidden under turbans,

swatches of brilliant crimson.
Their faces, also, shimmer
with light, with the peculiar
glee of infants, small children,

young women, a future
holding possibilities—
gossip—recipes—good
fish soup.

Cygnet

Flecks of blood bruise
Her window glass.

Her eyes refuse to close
On the familiar terror

Of unnatural desire,
And recurring loss.

What remains is grief.
Grief and a jewel of a heart,

A visceral kind of watch
That ticks and goes on ticking

As if it would never run down,
Although it is never wound,

Although it is never worn,
And the owner may be dead.

It lies boxed in a dresser drawer
Next to scarves, gloves,

Rings, nests of stockings,
Stacks of underwear.

She hears a car door slam.
At last somebody's home.

Her muscles relax. Her chills
Slacken. Her brooding darkness

Grows lighter. An indispensable
Dose of dreamless sleep

Is dependent on this
Chaste, paternal kiss.

Through the window, closed
And locked, a feather blows.

Film

This is how it begins: the hero
is traveling on a creaky, worn-
out train. He could be you, me,

anybody, traveling at that hour
when the day will soon slide off
its plate like an overcooked egg,

cars pick up speed and pass
one another with the roaring
madness of a river in spring,

and nothing has happened
to make any difference.
He regards, with ennui,

the South Bronx scenery—
gutted apartment houses waiting
for demolition. Each window,

a black hole, frames a man
or woman in dishabille,
ghostly elbows on the sill,

watching the trains pass,
watching our star, unaware.
He rarely looks out anymore.

A lifetime jerking along like
a streetcar! This is theatre
in five dimensions, cold

electrodes singeing the bank
in his brain, scenes springing out
pure and clean. With disbelief

he watches the chaos of reruns.
The disease known as memory is low-
brow, ordinary. There is no cure.

But what souvenirs—
pennies under a pillow, caves
carved out of sealed-over mines,

infected pools from which we drink.
Oh squinty-eyed mole,
seeker of scents and solutions,

can you find your way
around this imprecise system
without help? Without direction?

Here is a university
where records are vaunted,
where an unwilling student

searches for irretrievables
before what he fears,
coming upon him—clever

and sleek, a hex, a familiar—
clings until the grooves
of the brain are sponged clear

from the terror of blood
which will not stay warm,
even now the temperature

imperceptibly dropping
and resignation, sweet chemical,
rising to balance the fall.

Cells

My father, climbing stairs in tenements
to visit his parolees, frightened, a gun
in his holster he knew he'd never shoot.
Two hours a day packed into a subway.
Thirty years. Almost a life sentence.

My father, 74, incarcerated on the 14th
floor of a vast teaching hospital,
wearing striped pajamas and hooked
to a machine lit up like something
you drop quarters into. He raises
his head weakly and whispers,
P.J. you have a real hepatitis face.

Intensive Care: My mother, bending
over the bed, one of the tubes
sustaining him, blood and potassium
dripping in, maintaining
a proper electrolyte balance.

I'm leaving, riding back to Boston
on an old Pennsylvania Railroad car.
The air in here is greasy, poisonous.
We pass the Connecticut Sound. Three
bathers, heads teetering on a platter
of scummy water. A billboard
with this graffiti: *Rosie, I Love You.*

The word love, read in a jolt of wheels.
Astonishing. Ineludible. Like a blissful
couple, joined at the chest, thighs,
knees, kissing in the doorway
you're trying to exit through.

Waiting for Father in Pawling, N.Y.

I have been sitting at
the window since morning,
watching whirligig beetles

skim the surface of the pond
and listening to a high,
reedy song like the wind,

only higher, so high
the dog starts to moan
deep in his throat.

I am wearing a black felt
hat in memory of my uncle,
who drowned at City Island

sixty years ago. When you
arrive, we'll bury our
hearts (two small peach pits)

under the picnic table,
set out cold chicken, wine,
strawberries. We won't

speak of my solitude, how
fear for me makes you cry.
We won't wonder why your

left leg is dragging
more than ever. I'll say,
"I can't remember such

a good time, can you?"
After you leave I will
sit at the window and watch

whirling beetles wrinkle
the smooth skin on the pond.
I will think of your brother.

How he rented a rowboat,
brought a girl with him,
smoked a pipe all afternoon.

How he told her it was
the best day of his life.
How he was just

twenty when he waved and called
(it wasn't clear)
help and went under.

Solitude

It is too noisy. There is always
a grandmother wearing a bonnet

who gives advice, warnings. A sister
reminds me of the time I stole a

valentine from the five-and-dime. We
take heads, torsos, arms and legs from a

wooden trunk, feel fingers and toes as
if we are blind, try to fit pieces

together. The house is too small for
a family reunion. We walk to

Cape Kin, a projection of quicksand
and mosquitoes, always nearby. We

decide to tidy up. A vote is
taken. I am elected. They pack

dishes and food into huge wicker
baskets, wave goodbye. I sweep away

leaves, prune a few dead branches. It is
getting darker. It is getting very quiet.

Synechdoche by the Beautiful Sea

This is a snapshot of noses, only
noses, sticking above the surface
of the water. The waves roll in gently

festooned with flowers of foam before
they break without discomposure. The noses
come almost the whole way in, then return.

They do not touch the shore. So little
to go by. Yet it is all I have known.
It's a memory. It's the whole album.

If I could have seen a few eyes—ovals,
rectangles, or round ones full of noodles
for the loveless. Irises the color

of amethysts or bluebells, the color
of maple syrup. Hummingbirds balanced
in air, sipping nectar. The blurred, whirring

blades of a fan. A rich variety.
And then the chins, withdrawn, shy—the square
ones with fissures; the hair, faded old silk,

a nest to lie in, braided, looped, a rope
to swing from—lost—the torsos, all colors.
Much is happening that cannot be caught.

Perhaps the camera has not been perfected.
But the picture is clear, that's not the problem.
It's whatever I've missed, restricted to noses

like tea roses, or huge, confused, bruised, debauched—
the small portion I was allowed to see.
Even at that it was, at times, too much.

Jitters

Surely, not the first am I to nervous
thus in a hot parking lot—
ticketed or not—my head
hurting from the sun, from frets
watering my forehead, nose and armpits.
So long a search to find a single spot!

Three days ago in Central Square
great clouds of steam gushed
from the hood, a bilious green
fluid flooded the tar; the car's
repaired but not the frayed
splayed endings of my nerves.

Last night I dreamed my spirit-guide,
a young man in a t-shirt labeled
CIRCUMSTANCE, was pilfering, downstairs
in my residence, a few pitiful knick-
knacks with the aid of a plastic sack.
So! I am the victim of Circumstance!

No. I will not accept this excuse
offered from me to me, a white
narcissus in a grubby hand. Do I not
possess the silver key that slides
into the ignition slot? Who turns
the wheel? Who starts? Who stops?

Leaning against my declining vehicle
I practice deep-breathing, a technique
revealed by a yogi whose mustache
resembles the one Peter Sellers glued on
as a sleuth in *The Pink Panther*. I try
to find the still, null center of myself

around which insects whirr: leafhoppers,
fritillaries and other six-legged creatures—
rasped, ridged, hairy, smooth, pink, green,
spotted and brown—who wear their bones
outside of their bodies, their little lives
designed to chase intoxicating blooms.

Mendota River Inn

A man with a harmonica believes
he is entertaining.
Waltzing Matilda, waltzing Matilda,
you'll come a-waltzing Matilda with me . . .
We applaud politely.
In the music room, conversation
rustling over grieving faces,
lamplight revealing
features wrenched out of place.

Dr. Kavaney briefs us on
the latest medical statistics:
Every year   children
are born with a certain
terrible syndrome.
It is a matter of
the age of the mother.
"Some of you girls
may already be
too old to marry."

Is there no hope then, in modern times,
for men and women?
The discussion group is led
by Florence Chowder. Emily Cooley cries.
Dick Stromgrenz and Eric Lisle
lock in combat, have to be
torn from each other's arms.

Tonight our theme is not the usual cream
and magenta petals of love. We speak
only of the bud, how it resembles
solid silver. How it evades fingers
and thumbs, an inscrutable riddle
spilling into particles. How the particles,
fused once more, bloom into poisonous metal.

Irwin Tinowitz
switches on TV:
Welcome to the flu season. . . .
The nuclear accident that occurred on
Wednesday is a lot more complicated
than the public was led to believe.
A treacherous scorching bubble
is holding the experts at bay.

You can spend a great deal of time
with a stranger and not
come any closer, only you might.
Irwin and I pass a fertile hour
between the pansies and the peonies.
The primrose beds are edged
by a fringe of silence.

Tugboats are passing underneath the window,
heaving their ponderous bulk upstream.
In the morning they will be gone,
feuding only with each other
and the river, eluding memory.
Yet now they emit the great bellows
of a herd of Guernseys late for milking,
demanding their share of publicity.

Alice Bucci's husband beats her.
Her scars, she tells us, are
innumerable. "Leave him!"
I cry. She lowers her chin.
"Why?" she says, "Why?"

"Mind your own business,"
Felicia snaps at me. "You know
nothing of insecurity,
moving without a car,
dishwasher, silverware,
even furniture!"

Stuart Griddle unexpectedly
emits a primal scream;
beginning in his stomach
it bursts from his head—
an orgy of Roman candles.
He shivers and sobs.
We gather around to warm him
into acceptance of the animal
within. He is almost
strangled by our loving
efforts to convince him
it's his right to be born.

Our cauterized words reawaken at night.
They pinch like spiders.
The later it grows the livelier they are.
Marvelous treasures appear:
hoards of plovers' eggs and beach pebbles,
larkspur and lady-slipper,
Indian pipe and sticks of licorice.
In the morning we find a chair on its side,
a ping-pong paddle planted among the portulacas.

75

At breakfast, over orange juice,
Andy McSwee reads from the papers:
One in 400 marriages are between
carriers of cystic fibrosis. There is
a 25% risk that this tendency
will appear in their offspring.

Afterwards we sit in the game room.
It seems for the entire
weekend we have done nothing
but cry; everyone kisses
everyone goodby, except
for the harmonica player.
He refuses to stop.

And his ghost can be heard
as you ride beside the bill-a-bong,
"You'll come a-waltzing Matilda with me."

Irwin Tinowitz holds my shoulders,
looks at my lips and says,
"Alice and I agree
you are most deeply
disturbed of all."

He doesn't kiss me.
I am not speaking of the salt
taste of skin on skin.
I am not speaking of grunts,
groans, pants, wails, thumps
or moans. A trained guard dog
might stare in this fashion
through a chain link fence.
No band would be playing.
No one would dance.

After the Fiesta at Mendota River

Like the horse the farmer fed a little
less grain to each day, we believed
we were accommodating. We thought

we were feeling less pain. When my canoe
turned over in white water, my mind
flashing bright red—as if an entire

pot of geraniums had suddenly burst
into bloom—I was contemplating Edna,
her red hair, her preening stance,

and wondering what happens to a woman
who plans to become a legend—
who believes she is unique. Oh, ho!

A lesson to us all never to rise
above our positions of esteem between
registered nags and pedigreed sheep.

Who will accept our complaints?
Where can we go for advice?
We have lashed our mothers with sticks

and sent them into the woods, seamy
and sad-eyed as wisdom. Now they are
playing bridge by the water hole.

Their faces have been raised.
They are talking and talking.
They no longer know how to listen—

we tell them we are languishing,
we learn there is no sustenance—
although we are ravenous, we must

not forget we are only bony cattle
in a region picked clean by machines
rapacious as locusts and even more grotesque.

The truth is we are frantic, sniffing
and scurrying about like TV commercials
or chipmunks, a quick line across

the bottom of a screen; still we are
capable of hearing the music of wheels
and stars, and charming in our facilities:

rough beach and grasses leading down to the estuary.
What is it—this articulate privacy
passing between you, so necessary

to exclude us from? Clubs and guns, chainsaws,
bonfires of autumn afternoons, such
remarkable powers, singular joy

ringing and singing through the forests of the great
Western States. Trains rumbling across Indiana
and Kansas will not stop for the likes of us.

We are starving, we pray for a few wise
grains from your enormous combine. You let
them drop after we leave—among yourselves

a golden hill heaps up, until one of you
notices the sun is rising; it is
time for an aubade, it is time for morning prayers.

Men are no good, we said, and women are worse.
What remains? Monday, fur and feathers
in its jaws. Schools for unlearning the little

we once knew. From books we will gather
something—beside the point—foreboding,
despair, are left, and beyond all common sense

a fondness, sometimes human, sometimes
even a bird, even a pebble
is too much—a shackle, an unavoidable anachronism—

a sharp tooth—a dry mouth—a drop of honey.

Celebration

So drugged her lips stick together,
her words are blurred, and so thin that even
her heart is transparent, could break at any moment
like a wafer, Jane's mother imagines she's at a wedding
not lying in a slat-sided hospital bed.

She believes someone named Lisa is
getting married this evening. She'd like
to fix her hair, put on lipstick, go upstairs
where the crowd is, the drinking and kissing,
but she can't find her new dress.

It had silver lilies on the hem.
She is dreaming of a wedding with a cake
big as Texas and a Stetson-hatted bridegroom who
owns platinum and emerald mines. If only Jane's
mother could find her dancing dress!

The violets by her bedside are the same
shade as her eyes. She would wear them to
the wedding, she would look like an angel, if
she had her blue dress. Instead she rests her
halo of hair on the hospital pillow.

She says, "Jane, you go upstairs,
join in the dancing. The band, especially
the saxophone, is out of this world!" Jane laughs.
No, she is crying, as she waltzes with her weightless
mother in her ephemeral ice-blue dress.

Archaeology

FOR PASCALINE

The way it seizes you by the scruff of your neck—
You are unable to rise although you have
an appointment with your psychiatrist,
although you are already late.

Downstairs your children are quarreling.
The television snarls and whines.
Rapidly, with fading ink, you are writing in your notebook.

Through the floor, a shriek shoots like a spear.
You crash downstairs.
A bright light in the bedroom
illuminates a small white foot
snapped in a smear of blood.

This is not a clip snipped from a Hitchcock entertainment.
Quite simply, your cat is teaching her kittens how to hunt,
your daughter has slipped on the split
carcass of a baby rabbit.

Outside rain slides through leafless trees.
Everything is spongy and dark. With a flashlight
you show your young son a burial site.

He has always been competent with fishing
hooks and tools and cool as his former father.
You hand him a man's large shovel.

Each motion in your life is punishable.
A brick falling from a wall
can break your toe as you amble
down the driveway. A flick of a match
can level your home. He isn't quick.

He will not learn to forgive you this night,
or others. Skillful, deliberate,
he will grow like a species
of ivy, clinging to earth.

Researchers and statisticians
will lovingly, in the future,
surround him and his sister.
They will, like you,
spend much of their lives
hunting lost and buried bones.

Juice

It is a morning miracle, the chilled
blood defrosting, running once more
through the numb, the mute channels:

toast with margarine, tea-water
whistling in the kettle, round
white pill—Vitamin C—she imagines

aids in restoring the impeccable
balance needed to walk, the staggering
insouciance required to complete

a day by a small person with twisted
extremities and unyielding
stiffness in the elbows and knees,

who recollects her imperfections with shame,
hoping to come to her own forgiving,
a celebration like a wedding

with everyone smiling and a little
looped on pink champagne, who wears
a flowered cap, a wash dress, and ankle socks,

who in the heat of summer carries a blue
umbrella and crosses the street in a dazed
flutter against the light.